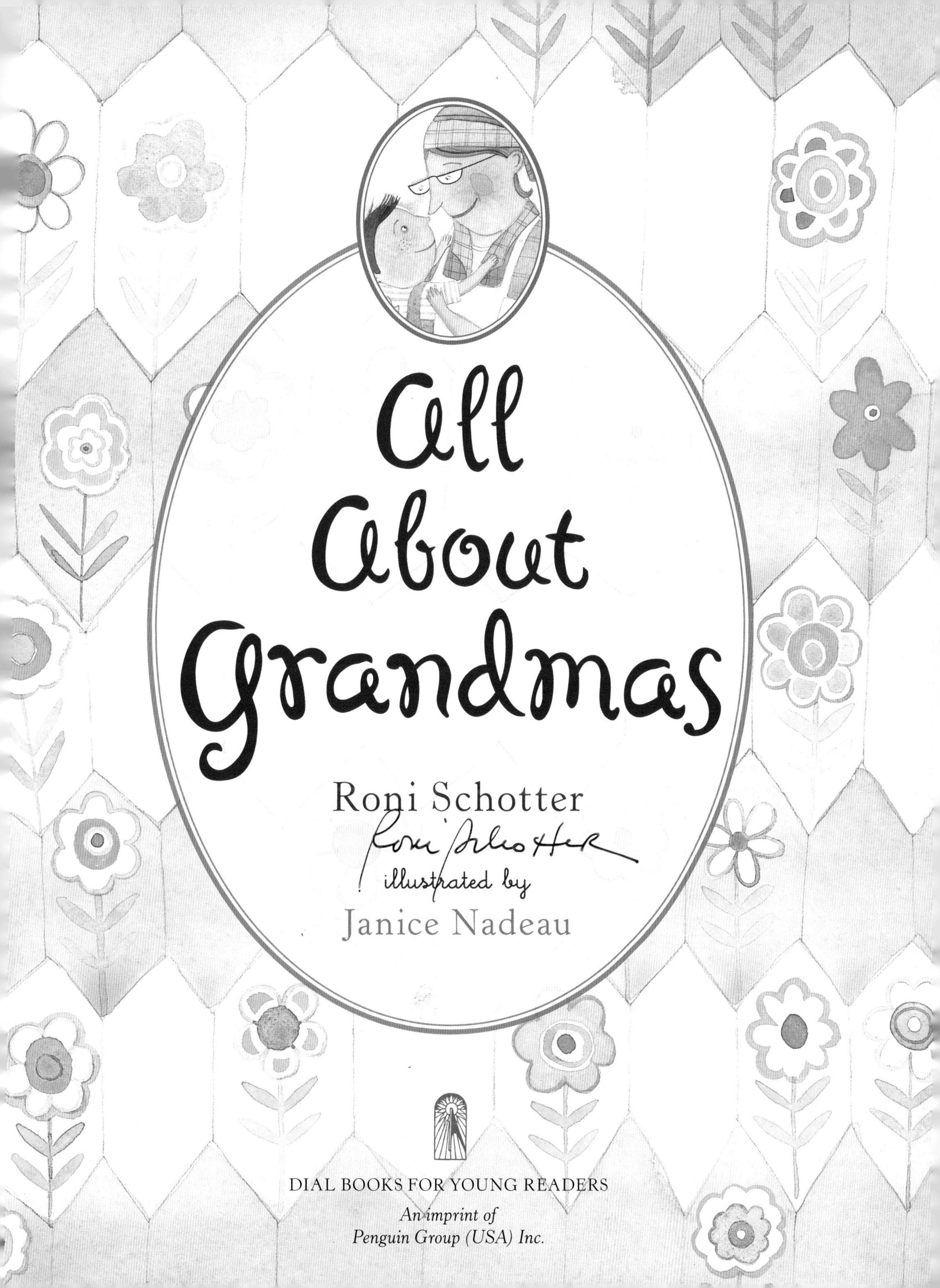

All About Grandmas

Roni Schotter

illustrated by

Janice Nadeau

DIAL BOOKS FOR YOUNG READERS

An imprint of
Penguin Group (USA) Inc.

To grandchildren and their loving grandmas everywhere,

but especially for Grandmas Wendy G, Fran C, Judy D, Judy B, Sally K, Jean G, Marisabina R, Annette W, Ilene E, Sandy G, Elizabeth E, Joanie F, Jane M, Kristin F-L, Kate R, Margery E, Shirley L,

and—all grandmothers-to-be!

—R S

To Felix's grandmothers
—J N

Dial Books for Young Readers
A division of Penguin Young Readers Group
Published by the Penguin Group • Penguin Group (USA) Inc., 375 Hudson Street, New York, New York 10014, U.S.A.
Penguin Group (Canada), 90 Eglinton Avenue East, Suite 700, Toronto, Ontario, Canada M4P 2Y3 (a division of Pearson Penguin Canada Inc.)
Penguin Books Ltd, 80 Strand, London WC2R 0RL, England
Penguin Ireland, 25 St Stephen's Green, Dublin 2, Ireland (a division of Penguin Books Ltd)
Penguin Group (Australia), 250 Camberwell Road, Camberwell, Victoria 3124, Australia (a division of Pearson Australia Group Pty Ltd)
Penguin Books India Pvt Ltd, 11 Community Centre, Panchsheel Park, New Delhi - 110 017, India
Penguin Group (NZ), 67 Apollo Drive, Rosedale, Auckland 0632, New Zealand (a division of Pearson New Zealand Ltd)
Penguin Books (South Africa) (Pty) Ltd, 24 Sturdee Avenue, Rosebank, Johannesburg 2196, South Africa
Penguin Books Ltd, Registered Offices: 80 Strand, London WC2R 0RL, England

CIP Data is available.

Published in the United States by Dial Books for Young Readers,
a division of Penguin Young Readers Group
345 Hudson Street, New York, New York 10014
www.penguin.com/youngreaders

Designed by *Irene Vandervoort*

Manufactured in China First Edition

ISBN 978-0-8037-3714-3

2 4 6 8 10 9 7 5 3 1

how to say Grandma

AROUND THE WORLD

Ouma - Afrikaans
Gjyshe - Albanian
Jaddah, Tetah - Arabic
Amona - Basque
Babka - Belarusen
Baba - Bulgaria, Serbia
Po Po - Cantonese Chinese
Elisi - Cherokee
Nai-Nai - Mandarin Chinese
Nokomis- Chippewa
Kookum - Cree
Baba - Croatian
Babicka - Czech
Bedstemor - Danish
Neske'e - Cheyenne
Grootmoeder - Dutch
Grandmother - English
Vanaema - Estonian
Mummo - Finnish
Grand-mère - French
Seanmhathair - Gaelic
Oma - German
YaYa, Giglia - Greek
Tutu - Hawaiian
Savta - Hebrew
Daa-dee-maa - Hindi
Nagyanya - Hungarian
Lola - Philippine dialect
Nenek - Indonesia
Aanaga - InupiaQ, Eskimo dialect
Obaasan - Japanese
Halmoni - Korean
Nonna - Italian
Nanna - Maltese
Bestemor - Norwegian
Babka - Polish
Vovo - Portuguese
Babushka - Russian
Bunica - Romanian
Babicka - Slovak
Stara Mama - Slovenian
Abuela - Spanish
Bibi - Swahili
Farmor - Swedish
Mino - Tagalog
AnneAnne or *Babaanne* - Turkish
Babusia - Ukranian
Dadi - Urdu
Bà - Vietnamese
Bubbe - Yiddish

They come in different shapes and sizes.
Silly ones wear disguises.
Some stride about in stylish heels.
Others glide through life on magic wheels.

There are jellying, jamming,
and pickling grannies,

plus a surprising number of
tickling grannies.

Some have a talent for fixing and mending,

others are expert at pretending.

Years of living have lined their faces
and turned their laps into cozy places.

And if you need to know more,
about whom they adore,
look in their eyes. . . .

If you haven't a grandma all your own,
perhaps you can find someone special on loan.
I have Jean who lives down the block.
She's nearly like family. I love her a lot.

And when I need to know,
who *she* loves so,
I look in her eyes. . . .

Nana, Nonna—their names are many:
Jean or Oma, Savta, Granny—
Nai-Nai, Tutu, Obaasan—
The names for grandmas go on and on. . . .

Lola, YaYa, Bunica,
Abuela, Bibi, Nagyanya,
Nokomis, Baba, Daa-dee-maa—
all ways of saying grandmamma.

Wherever they've come from,
whether near or so far,
you'll notice, like I do, how different they are.

There are cooking
grandmothers,

good-looking
grandmothers,

and *dancing*
grandmothers.

A few do yoga or tai chi to stretch.
Others sit and *schmooze* and *kvetch*—
(which means they like to gab and complain!).

One I know is a crossing guard.
Another knits sweaters by the yard.

There are nagging grandmas

and bragging grandmas,

some noisy,

some purry.

But no matter the grandma,
they all seem to worry!

Mischievous grandmas
pinch you and wink.

Book-loving grandmas
teach you to think.

They're great at explaining so many things,
like why a bat or a bird has wings;
or why, when you smile,
their hearts seem to sing.

Full of tales from long ago,
they have stories only grandmas know
about what they did when they were young—
the lives they've lived, the songs they've sung.
Just ask them . . . and they'll tell you one.

My Jean once wore bell-bottoms, tie-dyes, and tights.
She marched through the streets to win equal rights.

Other grandmas were groovy and danced rock and roll.
They can still twist their socks off and glide through the stroll.

Today grandmas work—in offices and stores—
then come home at night and do *still* more chores.

Work-at-home, stay-at-home, some love to travel.
Some work in courthouses, banging a gavel!

But whatever they work at, no matter where,
just like us grandkids, grandmas need care:

a hug or a kiss;
a cozy, soft chair;

someone to sing with;
a game they can share.

So tell them your secrets, by e-mail or phone.

Read them a story—one of your own?

Walk with them, talk with them, show how you've grown.

But remember, with grandmas
you *must* watch your back—
they tend to be ticklers and often attack!

They're playful and silly. They love to have fun.
They'll catch you for cuddles, then *laugh* when they're done.

You see, just like we do, *they* need to know,
who it is that loves them so.

So go . . .

grab the one *you* call grandma.
Act grown up and wise.
Show her your love—

it's there in your eyes.